ILLUSTRATIONS BY
THEA MOREAU
USING CANVA CONTENT

INTRAUTERINE INSEMINATION (IUI) IS A PROCEDURE THAT CAN HELP GROW FAMILIES AND HELP TREAT INFERTILITY. HOWEVER, EVERYONE'S FAMILY-BUILDING JOURNEY IS UNIQUE. AS A PROFESSIONAL IN THE FIELD OF INFERTILITY, I HOPE TO FURTHER EXPAND MY STORY COLLECTION TO REPRESENT THE MANY PATHWAYS THAT CAN BE TAKEN TO HELP YOU WELCOME YOUR ONE IN A MILLION.

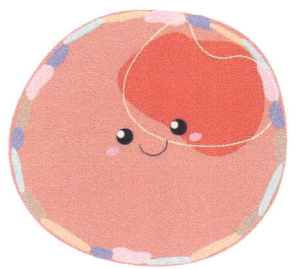

ONCE YOU'RE TUCKED INTO BED
AND THE LIGHTS ARE TURNED DOWN,

SEE, IT STARTED ONE MORNING, IN A KIND DOCTOR'S OFFICE.

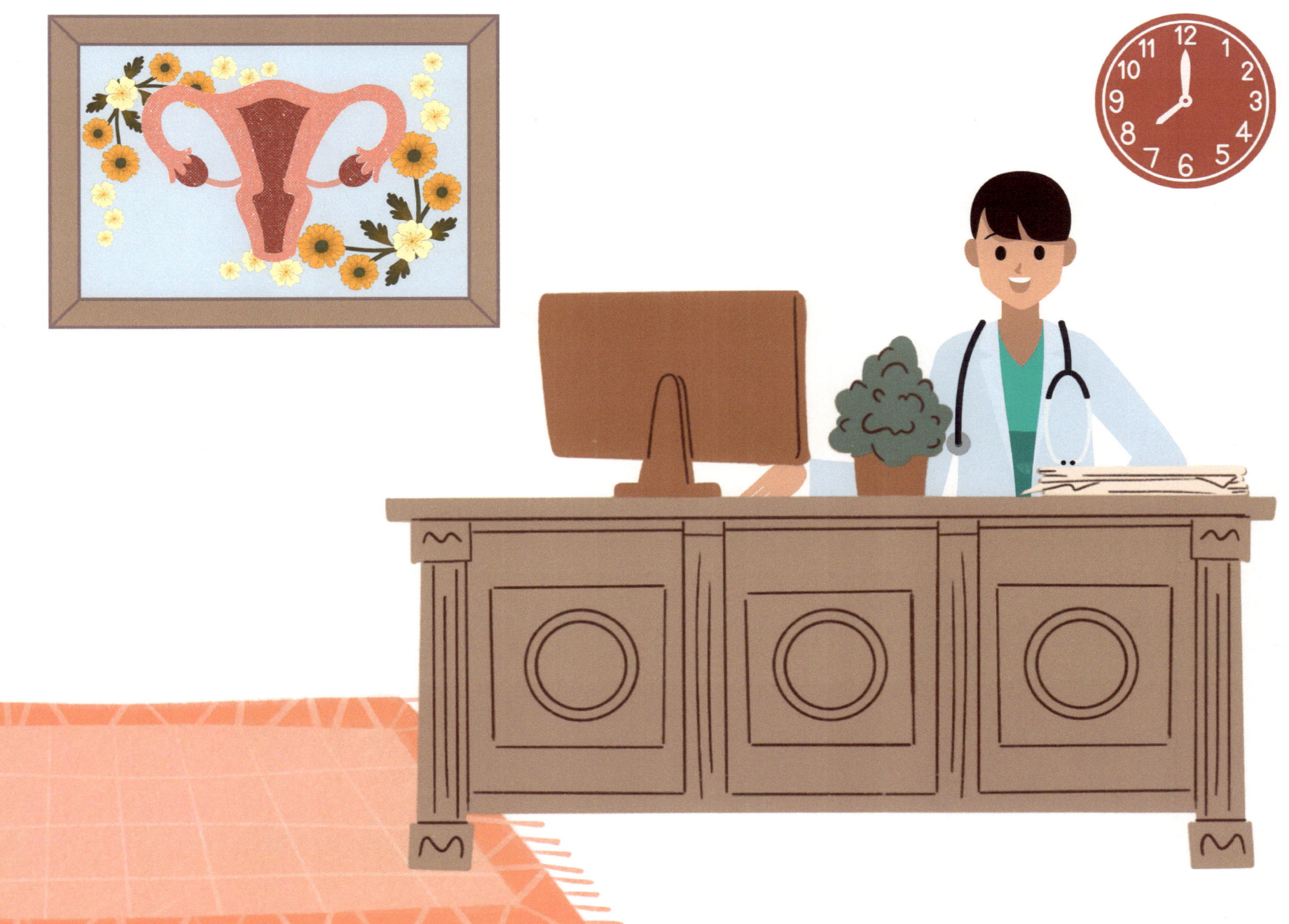

SHE WENT STEP-BY-STEP,

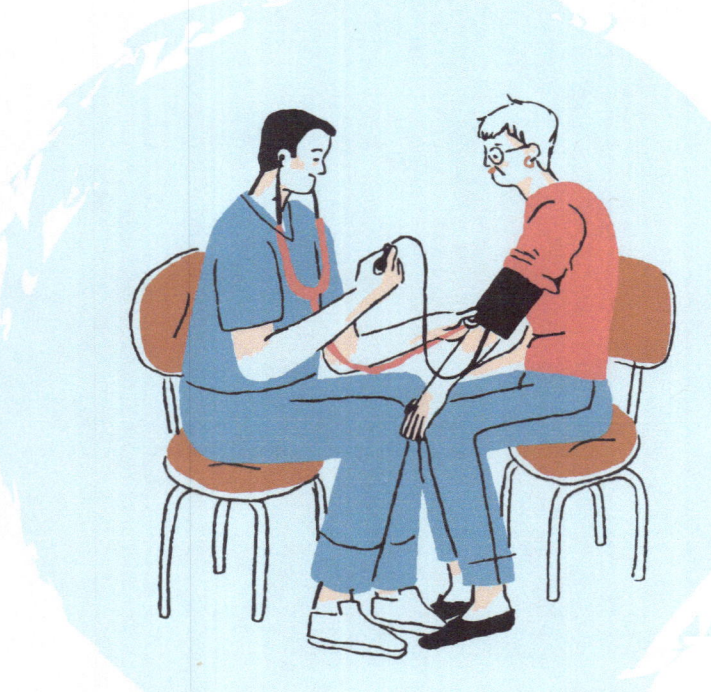

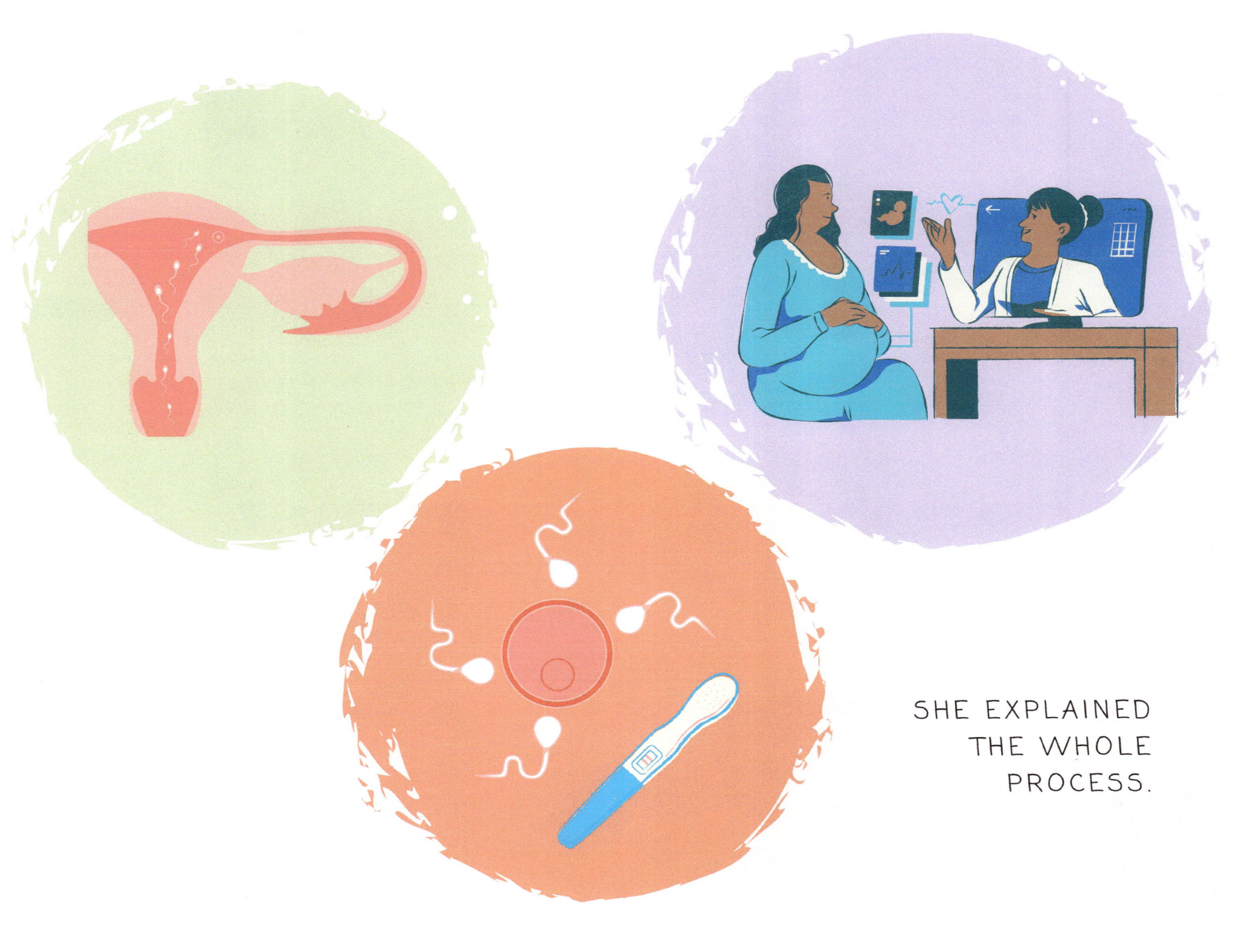

SHE EXPLAINED THE WHOLE PROCESS.

SHE GAVE US THE TOUR
AND INTRODUCED THE TEAM

WE COUNTED THE DAYS

AND PASSED ALL THE TESTS,

THEN WAITED FOR ONE EGG
TO WAKE FROM ITS REST.

WE RUSHED TO THE CLINIC, STRAIGHT TO THE LABORATORY.

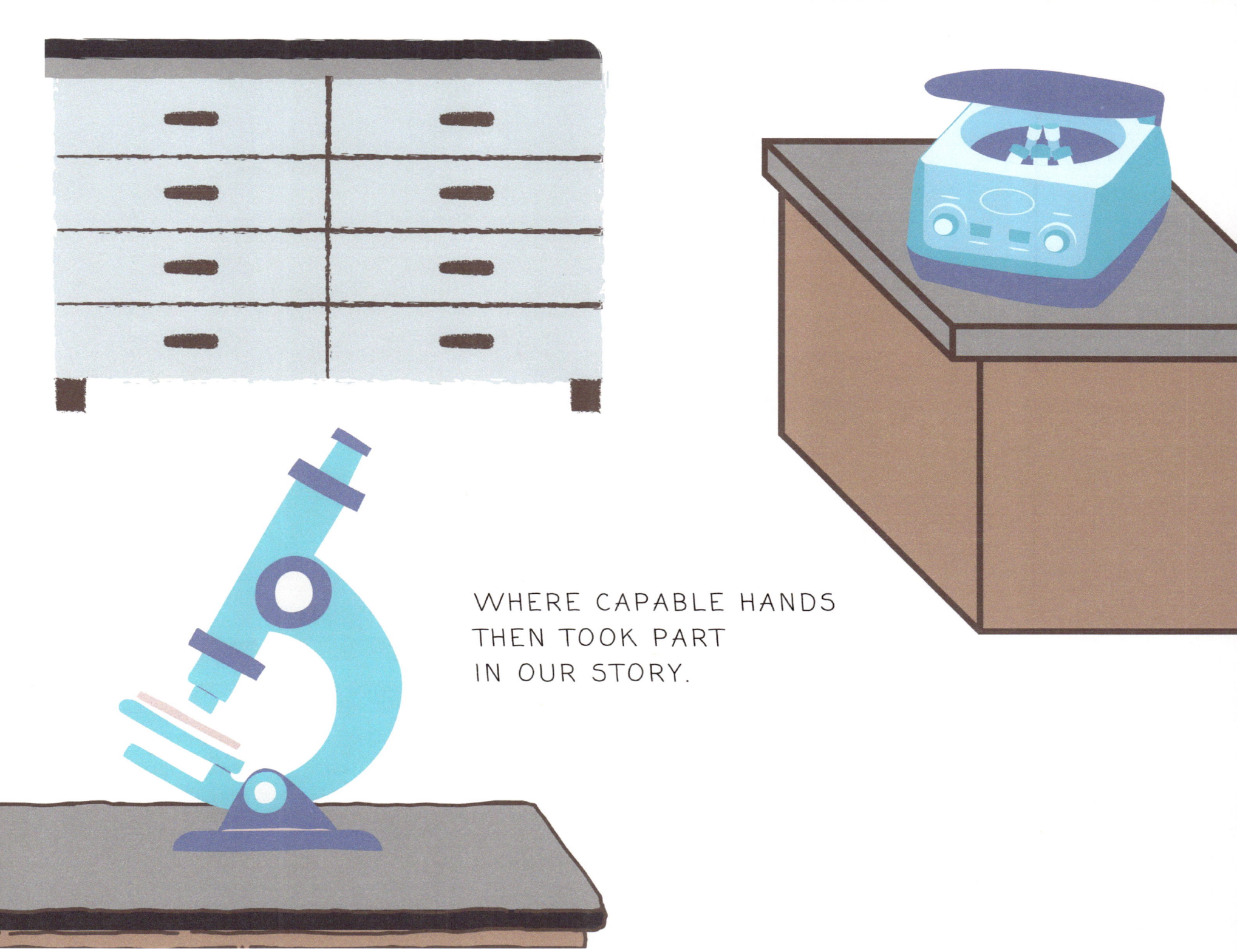

MILLIONS WERE WASHED THEN SENT ON THEIR PATH.

BUT IN THE END, ONLY ONE SPERM COULD REIGN.

THE DOCTOR INJECTED THE SPERM AND THEY

SWAM,

SWAM,

SWAM,

AT LAST, THE ONE IN A MILLION SPERM MADE IT THROUGH.

FASTEST TO THE EGG, TOGETHER THEY MADE YOU!

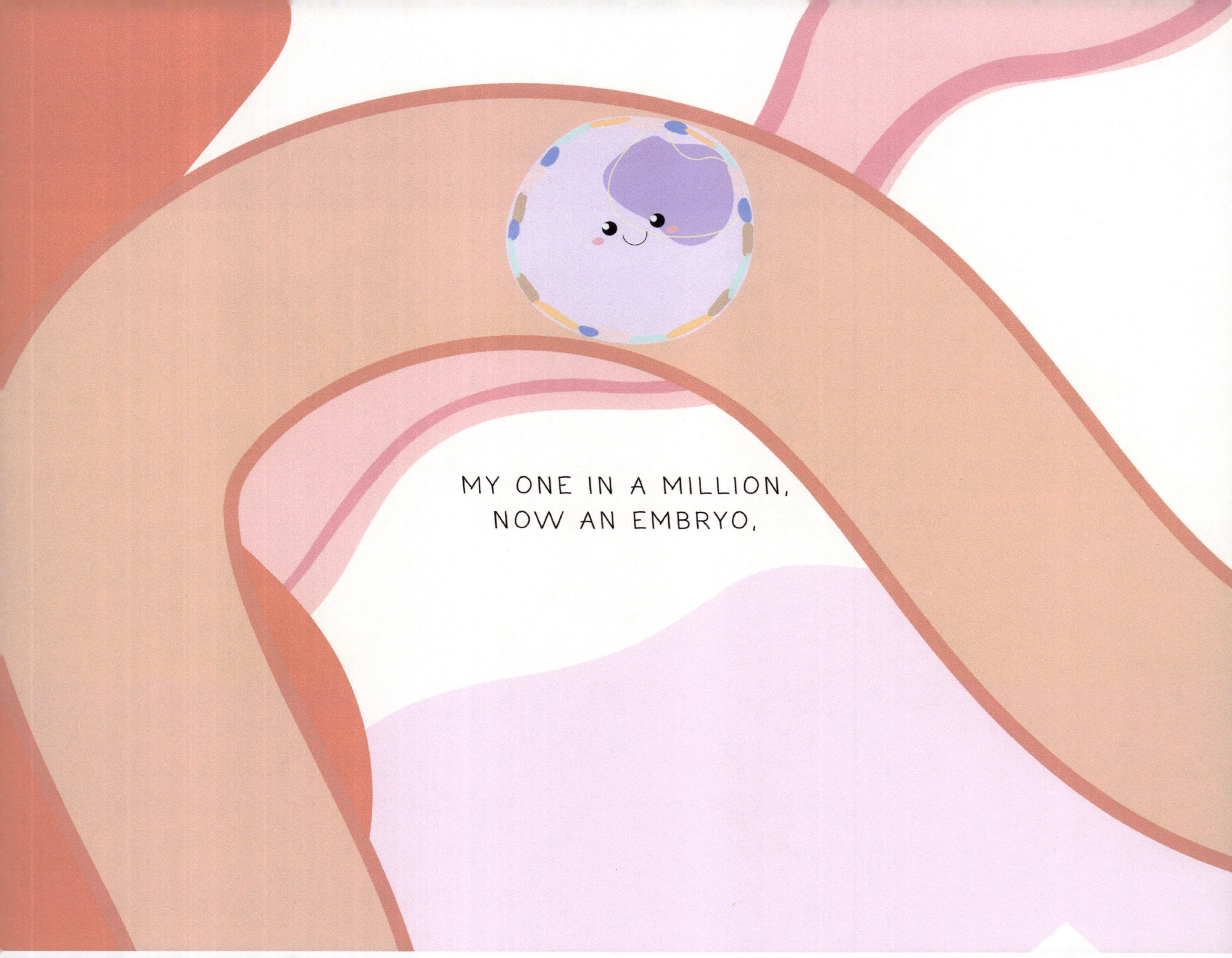

AND THEN, SOME TIME LATER, CAME YOUR FINGERS AND TOES.

WHILE OUT HERE WE SCRAMBLED AND TRIED TO GET READY.

AT LAST, THE DAY CAME WHEN YOU WERE DELIVERED

IN A ROOM FILLED WITH LOVED ONES AND MANY CAREGIVERS.

SO, DREAM BIG, MY LOVE, AND ALWAYS REMEMBER

THE END

www.ingramcontent.com/pod-product-compliance
Lightning Source LLC
Chambersburg PA
CBHW041819080526

44587CB00005B/146